T0157722

FOCUS ON THE GIVER,
NOT THE GIFT

FOCUS ON THE GIVER, NOT THE GIFT

Ten Strategies for **Building a** **Generous Church Culture**

Travis Moody

FOCUS ON THE GIVER, NOT THE GIFT
TEN STRATEGIES FOR BUILDING A
GENEROUS CHURCH CULTURE

iUniverse books may be ordered through booksellers or by contacting:

iUniverse
1663 Liberty Drive
Bloomington, IN 47403
www.iuniverse.com
1-800-Authors (1-800-288-4677)

ISBN: 978-1-5320-8178-1 (sc)
ISBN: 978-1-5320-8179-8 (e)

Print information available on the last page.

iUniverse rev. date: 08/30/2019

FOREWORD

Travis Moody and I first met in 2006 at a Crown Financial Ministries Annual Retreat. At the time, I served as CEO of Crown, an organization I cofounded with the late Larry Burkett. Travis shared how our ministry had drastically impacted his life and was a catalyst for his first published book, *Financial Breakthrough—God's Plan for Getting out of Debt*.

Travis had always dreamed of living a successful life. He played college football at Georgia Tech and graduated with an industrial engineering degree. Later he earned his MBA at Duke University. After a successful career with Fortune 500 companies, he made unwise decisions that led to a financial crisis for his family. He had no money, no income, and more than $100,000 in debt. On top of that, he had a huge mortgage on a home that he could not afford to live in, maintain, or even sell.

He and Carol had been married ten years, but this was the first time he had seen her cry because of something he had done. He felt like he had failed his wife, and he felt that God had failed him because his had always tithed. He could not understand why he wasn't prospering.

Carol suggested that they participate in a Crown small group study to learn what God says about money. As a result, Travis and Carol paid off more than $100,000 in debt in only three years. The last fifteen years, they have shared their story with thousands of others.

In 2008, Travis left a well-paid corporate executive career to serve full-time helping people learn biblical financial principles. He has worked successfully with dozens of churches and pastors. In 2011, he joined the Life Church as stewardship pastor with responsibility for growing generous givers called Vision Partners. In 2015, he formed the Lomah Consulting Group to help churches and individuals achieve their God-given purpose.

In this book, Travis shares ten proven strategies to help churches build a contagious culture of generosity. What I appreciate most is that this book encourages church leaders to focus on the giver and not the gift. As we help people become more like Christ, we create churches that will make an impact for God in generations to come. I am confident that this book will be a blessing to church leaders and will help your church achieve its God-given vision.

Howard Dayton
Founder Compass—Finances God's Way

PREFACE

What if you could increase the money given to your church between 15 percent and 20 percent? For a church that has a budget of $1 million, that could mean receiving an additional $200,000 a year. And what if you could receive that increase not just one year but every year for the rest of the life of your church? Imagine how you could impact your church and community with an additional $1 million every five years! How many lives could be transformed? How many ministries could be birthed? How many stories could be rewritten? The possibilities are staggering—although generating such a large sum of money may sound impossible. Well, it can be done. In fact, we have done it at my home church for the last eight years in a row.

Eight years ago, I met with the senior pastor and the executive pastor of my church for coffee. After we found our seats, well before the coffee cooled, they jumped in and asked me to serve the church in a new full-time role: stewardship pastor. I was honored but surprised.

I loved our church and had a lot of experience teaching people how to handle money God's way, but I didn't know what it meant to be a stewardship pastor. Neither did our pastors. This was a new role for the church with no job description. Instead, they asked me to help strategically support members with their personal finances and to determine what the role should look like.

At the time, the only stewardship pastor I knew was Gunnar Johnson at Gateway Church in Dallas, Texas. I reached out to Gunnar, and he invited me to the Christian Stewardship Network (CSN), where the few full-time stewardship pastors from around the US met together for an annual conference. Gunnar and the other CSN members gave me some thoughts on how to lead in my new role. I jotted down what I thought would be my new job description, shared it with my pastors, and received their blessing to go with it.

Over the last eight years, the Life Church has been my experimental laboratory to test different stewardship strategies. My experiments over the years have yielded ten successful strategies and just as many (maybe even more) to avoid. I will unpack each strategy in detail in the following chapters, but here are the ten strategies:

1. Communicate a compelling vision.
2. Have an effective offering moment during weekend services.
3. Preach on finances.
4. Invite tithers to become generous givers (Vision Partners).

5. Provide giving appreciation and follow-up.
6. Have intentional meetings with Vision Partners and potential Vision Partners.
7. Hold leaders accountable to a giving standard.
8. Offer regular stewardship education and coaching.
9. Teach generous giving to new members.
10. Assign a generous church champion/leader.

These ten strategies have helped produce outstanding financial progress in our church. In addition to the 15–20 percent increase in our annual budget each year, we found other intangible benefits:

- stronger relationships and deeper trust between pastors and givers
- easier conversations about money at church (those conversations are not weird)
- better member retention, as top givers rarely leave for another local church
- improved spiritual growth among members, as members strengthen their faith and personal finances
- greater unity among staff and lay leadership toward a common vision

I have used these strategies to help not only my church but several other churches that I have consulted with over the last eight years. Regardless of the size of your church, my hope is that the ten financial strategies unpacked in this book will help you realize similar or better results along your church stewardship journey.

ACKNOWLEDGMENTS

A special thank you goes to my senior pastors, John and Leslie Siebeling, for providing a church environment that allows me to grow spiritually, impact lives, and live out the dream God gave to me. And also to Pastor Mundo Meneses and the Life Church family for all you have done to support me personally and for allowing me to serve along with you. Finally, thank you to all the Vision Partners who give so much to move God's kingdom forward.

INTRODUCTION

I got a call from a church pastor who said, "I need your help. We need to increase our giving in order to accomplish the vision God has for our church." This is the struggle of almost every lead pastor I meet with. His or her dilemma can be summed up in these few thoughts:

- We need more money to fulfill our vision.
- I don't want to beg or pressure people to give.
- Talking about money feels awkward.
- I wish people were more generous, but I don't know how to go about helping people to be generous.

Pastors everywhere are frustrated when their congregations aren't generous. Most pastors think the solution is to focus on tithing each week or have a capital campaign. Some even feel that they have to put pressure on people or guilt them into giving. Still others try to convince their members to give in order to get financial blessings from God. None of these tactics will build a generous church, and many of these tactics are just plain wrong and unbiblical.

Scriptures tell us not to give out of pressure or guilt. God loves a cheerful giver. Even if you are able to increase giving through pressure, it is only a temporary fix. Eventually, the church will understand the routine and adjust their resources to accommodate the occasional guilt trip or special fundraiser. It actually hurts their ability to build a generous spirit.

Certainly there are blessings that come with living a generous life, but giving to get is the wrong attitude. So what is the answer? The solution is to build a culture of generosity. It's a long-term solution instead of a short-term fix.

How is this different from traditional capital campaigns? Typical stewardship consultants focus on raising funding through capital campaigns. They prepare pastors and leadership teams to motivate the congregation to give. Generally, in these cases, the focus is on the money and not the giver.

This book will encourage you to *focus on the giver, not the gift*. The primary objective is to execute God's great commission by making disciples. One standout characteristic of a disciple is that disciples are generous givers. They give freely of their time, talents, and money. There cannot be true discipleship without this characteristic. The goal of the principles outlined in this book is to help create an ongoing culture of generosity.

What is a culture of generosity?

A culture of generosity within a church creates an environment in which a significant number of members give willingly, cheerfully, sacrificially, and continually toward God's work.

People respond with this type of generous giving when they …

- are living overall healthy lives spiritually, relationally, physically, financially, and so on
- understand a clear and compelling church vision
- are engaged in the church vision
- are called/invited to support the church vision
- are appreciated for their generosity
- see real benefits from their giving
- trust how leaders handle money

A culture of generosity is not …

- a vehicle designed to raise more money for the church
- an extension of the business administration function
- a response to missed budgets or a building program
- a ministry to induce guilt about low giving by overwhelming people with scripture

Having a generous church is not something that just happens. It is something that has to be built and developed intentionally. I wrote this book as a resource to help pastors build a generous culture in their churches.

CHAPTER 1

Four Ingredients of a Contagious, Generous Church Culture

There is a story in the Bible that highlights what it takes to have a generous church culture. Moses was leading the Israelites out of bondage in Egypt to the Promised Land. As they traveled on their journey, the LORD said to Moses, "Tell the Israelites to bring me an offering. You are to receive the offering for me from everyone whose heart prompts them to give … Then have them make a sanctuary for me, and I will dwell among them" (Exodus 25:1–2, 8).

Moses gathered the men skilled at building and gave them the offerings the people brought to build a sanctuary for God. Meanwhile, the people continued to bring offerings to the builders. They brought so much that the builders went to Moses to say, "The people are bringing more than enough for doing the work the LORD commanded to be done." Moses responded by commanding the Israelites to stop giving offerings because they had more than enough to do all the work (Exodus 36:1–7).

Can you imagine getting in front of your church and commanding everyone to stop giving because you had more than enough to do the work? Probably not. This story highlights four key ingredients necessary to create a contagious, generous church culture. These ingredients are the basis of the ten strategies I will discuss in chapters 4 through 14.

1. A Clear and Compelling Vision (Exodus 25:1–2, 8)
   People give to vision. Givers are inspired when they invest in a cause bigger than themselves. I spoke with a pastor who had a really compelling vision. But when I spoke with members of his leadership, none of them could explain his vision to me. The vision wasn't clear. The Israelites had a clear, compelling vision—to build a tabernacle for the Lord. When people have a clear and compelling vision, they are more likely to carry out the desired action.

2. A Commitment to Good Stewardship
   The second ingredient in a culture of generosity is a commitment to good stewardship.

   From what you have, take an offering for the Lord. Everyone who is willing is to bring to the Lord an offering of gold, silver, and bronze (Exodus 35:5).

In order to give something, a person must possess it. That implies that givers must be good stewards over what God has already given them. Stewardship precedes generosity. The people who gave were good stewards over their things, so when it came time to give, they had the resources to give.

All of us need more education on finances, but few of us seek it on our own. Some of us are too embarrassed to ask for advice or lack motivation because our situation isn't that bad. Good stewardship requires managing our lifestyles so that we are in a position to give. When we are better stewards, we have less stress and better marriages and are better able to fulfill our God-given purpose.

3. A Commitment from Leadership
   Exodus 35:27 gives us our third ingredient.

   The leaders brought onyx stones and other gems to be mounted on the ephod and breastpiece.

   The people were generous because they saw their leaders were generous.

   John Maxwell is often quoted as saying, "Everything rises and falls on leadership" (John Maxwell, *The 21 Indispensable Qualities of a Leader*, Nashville: Thomas Nelson, 2007). It comes down to leaders. When leaders of the church worship, the people worship. When leaders of the church give, the people will too.

The church needs leaders who carry the mantra that says, "If it's going to be done, then it's up to us as leaders." Church leaders can't think, *I wish others would help*, but must embrace their roles as leaders, lead the way, and commit to raising the funds needed. This will set the tone so that others will follow.

4. A Call to Discipleship

    In Exodus 32, God had just delivered the Israelites from slavery in Egypt and parted the Red Sea for their escape. They arrived at Mount Sinai for further instruction from God. Moses went up Mount Sinai to hear from God and received two tablets with commandments from God. The Israelites felt Moses had been gone too long, so they pressured Aaron to build them a golden calf to worship as their god. Moses returned to see the Israelites out of control worshipping the idols, so he stood at the entrance of camp and said, "Whoever is for the Lord, come to me."

    In true Old Testament fashion, Moses told the people who had come to him to take their swords and kill all the troublemakers leading the Israelites astray. I'm not suggesting we go wiping out all those who are troublemakers. Although we may feel like it sometimes, we can't just wipe out all the troublemakers in our church.

    So, what does this have to do with generosity in Exodus 36? The key lesson is that the only people left in Exodus 36 were those who made a commitment that they were for the Lord. Stewardship is about making disciples. The giving continuum table below is a view of the typical church based on their level of giving. I will unpack these four groups more in chapter 3, but here I would like to make the point that the objective of the financial ministry is to disciple people to deeper levels of generosity. This is done by consistently inviting people to make a decision to follow God in the area of their finances.

Giving Continuum

Seeker	New	Immature	Maturing
Non-Giver	Sporadic Giver	Regular Giver	Generous Giver
0%	1-2%	3-9%	=>10%

CHAPTER 2

Discipleship Process—
Like Riding a Bike

I had the privilege of teaching each of my four kids how to ride their bicycles. I would run behind them holding the back of the seat until they had the confidence to ride freely on their own. It was a thrill for them and for me. There is nothing like the feeling of riding a bike on your own with the wind in your face. It is one of life's greatest enjoyments.

God has a similar experience He wants those in your church to enjoy. It's just as thrilling as learning to ride a bike but also just as scary. It's the freedom of living a generous life. There is nothing more thrilling than living a generous life, yet few people ever experience it.

The truth is that life doesn't have meaning until we learn to give it away to others. Bill Gates, one of the richest men in the world, pledged to give away 95 percent of his net worth. Bill and Melinda Gates said, "It's the most fulfilling thing we've ever done." They realized that it's when we give ourselves to something bigger than we are that we find true fulfillment.

Learning to live a generous life is similar to learning to ride a bike. Just like my kids went through stages in order to become bike riders, every giver typically goes through four stages in order to experience a life of generous giving.

Step 1: Training Wheels

To teach my kids to ride a bike, I would start them with training wheels. Training wheels helped them gain confidence in their ability to steer and balance the bike within a safe environment until they were skilled enough to do it on their own.

Almost everyone starts their bike-riding journey with training wheels. It builds their confidence and allows them to build up the necessary skills so one day they can ride freely on their own. The objective is not to ride with training wheels forever, but most of us would never have learned to ride a bike without help from training wheels.

Training wheels in the process of becoming a generous giver are called tithing.

Most Christians are familiar with the term tithe but may not understand what it really means. The term *tithe* literally means "a tenth part," just like the word half means 50 percent or a quarter means 25 percent. Tithing is bringing the first 10 percent of a person's income to God through a local church. Tithing is a systematic way of giving. It provides a clear benchmark for action.

Even riding with training wheels can be scary to the newest of bike riders. Similarly, giving even a small percentage of income to God is intimidating for many Christians. Even though most Christians say that they tithe, only about 9 percent actually do. The average giver gives about 2.5 percent to their church. ("New Study Shows Trends in Tithing and Donating," Barna.com, April 14, 2008).

Every pastor dreams of having a church full of skilled bike riders (i.e., givers) yet is often frustrated when 90 percent of the church won't even ride with training wheels (i.e., tithe).

So many critics want to argue the biblical positions on whether Christians should tithe. Although I believe the Bible supports the principle of tithing, it's senseless to argue the point because I would recommend tithing even if the Bible was silent on the subject.

It's no different from when I recommended to my financial coaching clients that they save 10 percent of their income. Nowhere in the Bible does it suggest to save 10 percent, but I encourage it because it is a basic habit that leads to financial success.

Ironically, no one ever challenges me when I suggest Christians should save 10 percent for the future. Why? Because saving still feeds the selfish desire to be rich. In contrast, tithing starves the basic selfish desire to live a me-first life.

People make a huge deal out of such an insignificant thing. Here is what I mean. In any other area of life, most people consider 10 percent to be insignificant. Most people don't get excited when there is a "10 percent off" sale at their favorite store. People usually don't complain if they are asked to pay 10 percent in taxes or a 15 percent tip to a server at a restaurant. The only time 10 percent seems to become a big deal is when Christians are giving it to the church.

The decision to tithe is a spiritual issue, not a financial issue. Tithing is a critical step toward helping givers learn to live a generous life.

Tithing is a tangible way to show God honor, love, and trust. It teaches us to make God a financial priority. It builds faith in God and draws the heart closer to Him. As spiritual muscles strengthen, the giver is prepared, positioned, and purposed to give more.

Tithing is not the end goal for Christians. The end goal is to become a generous giver. Just like most of us would never have learned to ride a bike without training wheels, most Christians will never know the freedom of generous giving unless they first practice the principle of tithing.

Step 2: Maintenance

When I taught my kids how to ride bikes, I also had to teach them how to take care of their bikes. They needed to know how to put air in the tires and occasionally repair a flat or change the brake pads. They also needed to make sure to store their bikes in the right place so that they didn't get stolen or run over by a car. It was important to take care of their bikes in order to enjoy the bike rides.

FOCUS ON THE GIVER, NOT THE GIFT

For Christians, this is a call to good stewardship. Just like taking care of the bike is necessary in order to ensure long-term enjoyment of bike riding, being a good steward of your personal finances is just as necessary to becoming a generous giver.

Paul said, "I have learned the secret of being content in any and every situation, whether well fed or hungry, whether living in plenty or in want" (Philippians 4:12 NIV). The key is that contentment and good stewardship can be learned. No one is born with it. Instead, it is a sign of spiritual maturity.

Good stewardship is spending less than one earns and wisely investing the difference.

It's impossible to be generous without stewardship, and it's impossible to be a good steward without generosity. By that I mean good stewardship is necessary in order to have the resources to be generous. On the other side, it is impossible to be a true steward of God's financial resources without also giving generously toward things that are important to God. Stewardship and generosity are opposite sides of the same coin. There can't be one without the other.

Givers can't be generous without dealing with the desire to want more. We will always want more than what we earn. That's why so many highly paid athletes go broke. No matter how much money we have, there is always more stuff to spend it on.

It is important to incorporate personal finances as a part of the church education experiences. Later, I will discuss ways of teaching good stewardship in your church.

Step 3: Removing the Training Wheels

As I mentioned before, tithing is not the end goal. It is only a step toward the end goal of generosity.

Jim Collins wrote a book called *Good to Great*, and in it he commented that the enemy of great is not bad but good. Bad companies know they are not great, so they are motivated to improve, but being good can keep companies from being great. These companies slowly become bad companies before eventually failing to exist.

Overly focusing on tithing can actually be counterproductive to building a generous church culture. Just as having a goal to be a good company becomes the enemy to becoming a great company, focusing on tithing only can become the enemy of generosity. Tithing is a critical step in achieving a more important goal—experiencing the freedom of generous giving. Tithing is good but not great. When tithing is seen as the end goal, we miss out on the larger goal of generosity.

The biblical standard for giving is generosity, which is usually so much more than 10 percent. In most cases, not tithing reflects a lukewarm heart toward God. The truth is everything we have belongs to God, not just 10 percent but 100 percent.

I love the way Jesus talked about tithing in Matthew 23:23 (NLT). He said, "You should tithe, yes, but do not neglect the more important things." Jesus's response shows us that tithing is just a baby step for Christians.

Just like riding with training wheels is not the goal, tithing is not the goal. It's just the beginning.

After a while of riding with training wheels, my kids were able to eventually ride their bikes without thinking so much about it. They were safe and, for the time being, had some fun. The downside is that they couldn't go very fast. Eventually, the thrill of bike riding with training wheels wore off. This wasn't exactly what they envisioned when they asked my wife and me to give them a new bike. Their goal was not just to ride the bike with training wheels. The goal was to be able to ride freely on their own as fast as the bike would allow them to go.

So, inevitably, I would eventually hear them say, "Daddy, can you take off my training wheels?" Taking the training wheels off was scary for them, but it was a necessary step in the process of them learning to ride a bike. Riding without training wheels was more challenging and required a little more ability. I would run alongside them holding the back until they could ride themselves. Some took longer than others, but all my kids eventually got it. It seemed like one day it clicked in their minds that they could ride on their own, and they took off.

We remove the training wheels in developing generous givers by inviting tithers to begin giving an offering above the tithe.

Where a tithe amount was determined for us, an offering is anything a person chooses to give over and above the tithe.

Most people who actually tithe and become good stewards usually move on to the third step pretty easily if they are invited to give more and provided with a compelling vision.

It is important to encourage people who tithe to give generously above their tithe toward the vision of the church.

When we invite people to give offerings above the tithe, we are asking the same question that Moses asked the Israelites, "Whomever is for the Lord, come with us."

We have to be bold to invite people to grow in the area of financial generosity. I call the community of believers who accept this invitation Vision Partners. I will discuss Vision Partners more throughout later chapters.

Step 4: Free Riding

It was a thrill for me to watch my kids grow into bike riders. When they finally got it, they were zooming down the street, yelling, "Look, Dad! Look at me!" Eventually they were popping wheelies and riding with no hands. It was fun for me to see how much they enjoyed the freedom of bike riding without training wheels.

Just like the goal for my kids was not to ride forever with training wheels, the goal is not to have people give when they are asked or prompted to give. The goal is to grow people to the place where they enjoy the freedom that comes with generous giving.

When you are maturing in the area of your finances, you no longer need to be handheld in your giving. God presents opportunities to partner with Him financially to see His work done on earth and in people's lives. Our question becomes, "God, what role would You like me to play in meeting this need?" Then, we are able to hear clearly from God and act in obedience with generosity.

Generosity is an overwhelming characteristic of God. John 3:16 (NIV) says, "For God so loved the world that he gave his one and only Son, that whoever believes in him shall not perish but have eternal life." God is creation's original giver and the most generous being ever! If we are to reflect His character to the world, then we should also have a generous spirit. There is no such thing as a stingy Christian. That would be an oxymoron.

Generosity is simply not about how much money we give. It's about the attitude of our hearts toward the money. Generosity is a mind-set, an attitude, and a lifestyle. It releases blessing in our lives and allows us to partner with God to significantly impact the lives of others.

I believe if more people only knew the joy that comes with giving, they would give more. Acts 20:35 (NIV) quotes Jesus saying, "It is more of a blessing to give than to receive." That sounds backward to most of us.

I know if I had a choice to either lack the means to meet my basic needs or have an abundance that not only meets my needs but also positions me to help others, my preference would be the latter. Blessing others through our giving is so much more enjoyable.

My wife, Carol, and I were on a trip out of town and staying at a hotel. I heard a knock on the door from the maid, but Carol was inside sleep. I asked for a couple towels and told the maid we didn't need cleaning service today. A short moment after I closed the door, I had a thought that I should give her a tip even if she didn't clean the room. I went and found the young lady going to the next room.

I hadn't noticed it before, but when I went to give her a tip, I saw that the young lady was pregnant. I handed her the forty dollars cash I had in my pocket and thanked her for the towels. I'm not sure whether the money meant a lot to her or not, but it meant a lot to me. It felt good to show generosity. When I give, I get excited. I left that young lady and floated back to my room. I'm sure my feet never touched the ground. It's true. It is more of a blessing to give than it is to receive.

We teach generosity not so we can get more from our congregations. We teach it to get more for them. We desperately want everyone we encounter to experience the pure joy that comes with living a generous life.

CHAPTER 3

Typical Church Profile

I assess churchgoers in the typical church from two perspectives: financial status and spiritual maturity. The combination of these two dynamics drives their level of giving. Each of these typical church perspectives has four different people groups. The four people groups based on financial status are struggling, surviving, successful, and surplus.

I have been able to compile giving data from churches over the years to create a model of the typical church. There are many variations in churches, but these descriptions are my best attempt at describing what I see in the typical church.

Struggling

The people in this group have no disposable income. They are likely to be dependent on others just to take care of basic needs. They may be going without or having a difficult time taking care of basic needs such as food, transportation, housing, utilities, and medical care. They are likely to have significant debt. It's important to know that struggling is not directly tied to a person's income level. A person could be struggling due to the financial circumstances they were born into. Other times, people actually have what is considered high income for the part of the world in which they live, but they struggle financially because of poor personal financial decisions.

Surviving

This group is just one missed paycheck from struggling. They live paycheck to paycheck. They don't have money saved and are probably burdened with a lot of debt. They are getting by but worry a lot about their finances.

Successful

This group is doing okay financially. They have decent incomes and tend to live a middle- to upper-class lifestyle. They wouldn't think of themselves as rich, but they enjoy a good lifestyle with very little worry about how they will pay bills and meet their basic needs.

Surplus

This group is wealthy. They may or may not work. If they do work, they probably run a business of their own or hold a high-profile job. They have a high net worth. They are often sought out to give to charitable organizations.

Financial Status Profile for a Typical Church

Financial Status	% of Church	% of Total Church Giving
Struggling	10–15%	1–5%
Surviving	15–25%	10–15%
Successful	35–45%	20–30%
Surplus	10–15%	50–60%

The second perspective for a typical church is based on spiritual status. This perspective also has four people groups: seeker, new believer, immature believer, and maturing believer.

Seeker

Some pastors make the mistake of thinking they just need to get everyone to tithe. That is only possible if there are no unbelievers or seekers in your church. If you have no seekers in your church, then you have a huge problem. The church is God's primary tool to reach unbelievers. You can only reach them if they are visiting your church.

If the church is doing its job of sharing the Gospel with people who do not know Jesus, then there are destined to be people in the church who do not give to the church. Understand that it is unrealistic to expect unbelievers to give. Why would they give if they do not believe?

If you are a growing church, you will always have a significant number of attendees who aren't believers and who don't give or give very little. That's got to be okay because those are the people you are trying to reach.

You will not reach them by talking to them about giving money. You reach them by creating an environment where they can begin to have a new or closer relationship with Jesus.

New Believer

This group consists of new converts who have never been taught how to handle money God's way and may be suffering financially because of it. They do not understand giving. All of us at some point were part of this group. We believe, now what? We begin the journey of aligning our lives to our new beliefs.

If you combined this group and seeker groups in a growing church, you will find about 30 percent of the church, and together they represent very little of the giving (0 to 5 percent).

Immature Believer

In some churches, this group can be as high as 60 percent of the church. But because they do not tithe consistently, their giving represents less than 25 percent of the total church giving.

People in this group can have an entitlement and me-first mentality. This immature group could be very vocal and demanding. You have to be careful not to give this group a commanding voice in the church. Certainly you have to be careful not to have them as part of the leadership. Their spiritual immaturity can create division and prevent the church from moving forward.

There is a great example of this in the Bible (Numbers 13 and 14 NIV). As Moses was leading the Israelites out of Egypt and into the Promised Land, he sent twelve spies out to check out the land before they entered it. Two of the spies came back with a positive report and said, "We should go up and take possession of the land, for we can certainly do it." The other ten spies were immature spiritually and came back with negative reports. They reported, "We can't attack those people; they are stronger than we are." These ten spiritually immature spies spread among the Israelites a bad report about the land they had explored. The people believed the negative reports, and it prevented the Israelites from moving forward into the land God had for them.

Immature believers may have worked their way into key roles in the church. Their rise to church leadership could be because of family affiliation, their position in the community or corporate world, or simply because they have been in church for a long time. None of these things in themselves, however, are indicators of spiritual maturity. On the other hand, one clear indication of spiritual immaturity is giving less than 10 percent of their income to their church.

If you ask an immature believer, they would probably say that they tithe even though they clearly do not.

I conducted a survey of members at a church and asked questions like, "How many times a week do you attend church?" and "How often do you serve in a ministry?" One of the questions was, "Do you tithe 10 percent of your gross income to your local church?" The results baffled me. It seemed on most questions, people responded with total accuracy, but when it came to the tithing question, the results were astonishing. Seventy percent of the members said that they were tithers, yet only 10 percent of the members gave at least $800 per year. This was shocking to me since the average annual income in this church was around $42,000. It was an anonymous survey, so there was no benefit to lying. Why would people lie about this question and not the other questions?

It baffles me. I really don't think they are just blatantly being untruthful. An article in the *New York Times* explains how if you tell yourself something long enough, your mind begins to believe it as truth (Dupree, "Can you Become a Creature of Habit?"). This could explain why immature believers respond the way they do when asked about their giving. It seems that they have convinced themselves that they are tithers even when they are not.

I was coaching a couple that was adamant that they tithe. I didn't even bring up the subject. They did. But as I looked at their financial information, I saw that they had earned $160,000 but had given only $7,000. When I pointed this out, they seemed confused. They were adamant that something had to be wrong with my math because they believed that they were tithers.

I have conversations about this almost every week. Spiritually immature people have blinders on when it comes to their finances. But because we teach tithing in a clear and noncondemning way, it opens up doors for us to disciple people. As I noted earlier, it's not a financial issue as much as it's a spiritual issue. If you do not teach this regularly and have tithing as an expectation, you will miss out on key opportunities to disciple your church.

The larger the population of immature believers is, the harder it is for the church to make progress. As I mentioned, you will likely always have the 30 percent who are seekers or new, so your goal should be to reduce the population of immature givers and increase the population of maturing givers. Following the strategies listed in this book will encourage some in this group to mature spiritually and prevent others from entering into this group.

A recommended strategy such as having a giving standard for leadership will make it uncomfortable for immature believers to remain immature in your church. It may seem harsh, but you want them to either mature or leave. If they choose not to mature and to leave, your church will be better off for it. The result of these three things is that immature givers will become a smaller percentage of your church.

Maturing Believers

These are the people in the church who are at least tithing. In the typical church, this group represents only about 10 percent of the church but gives 70 percent or more of the resources. Remember giving is an indicator of spiritual maturity. In general, this group represents the more spiritually mature people in the church. They are usually the more positive and the more engaged people in the church. They love God, the leadership, and their church. They are the most desirable people for a pastor to lead. Yet they are also the most overlooked group when it comes to discipling financially.

When a church is tithe focused and not generosity focused, they ignore this group. This group tunes out, thinking you are not talking to them, because they are already tithing, but they perk up with excitement to hear a message on generosity. When the subject is generosity and not tithing, it's as if they are finally hearing their heart's song. Developing this group will make the largest impact both financially and spiritually on your church. The obvious goal in a generous church culture is to grow this group.

Giving Data by Spiritual Level		
Spiritual Level	**% of Church**	**% of Total Church Giving**
Seeker	10–15%	0–1%
New Christians	10–15%	0–5%
Immature Believers	60–80%	15–25%
Maturing Believers	10–20%	70–80%

Financial and Spiritual Level Matrix

The table below is a matrix that shows all possible combinations of spiritual and financial groups in the typical church and the percentage of total church giving that is received from each group combination. The top row contains the financial groups, while the far left column has the spiritual maturity groups. When you look at these two characteristics together, it reflects the typical church-giving pattern.

Giving by Group as a Percent of Total Church Donations

	Struggling	Surviving	Successful	Surplus
Seeker	0%	0%	0%	0%
New	0%	0%	1%	1%
Immature	0%	3%	9%	12%
Maturing	2%	11%	23%	38%

As you see from the table, most income (74 percent) comes from maturing members, although they only represent 10 percent of the church. Even though seekers and new believers represent about 30 percent of the church, very little of church giving (less than 2 percent) comes from this group no matter their financial status. Immature givers account for about 60 percent of the church but only about 24 percent of the giving.

CHAPTER 4

Tactics for Developing Generous Givers from Each Giver Type

B elow is a matrix of the different groups and different tactics that help develop each group. Each tactic targets a particular group in your church based on their financial status and spiritual maturity.

Stewardship Tactics by Financial Status and Spiritual Maturity

	Struggling	Surviving	Successful	Surplus
Seeker	Stewardship Education Biannual sermon	Stewardship Education Biannual sermon	Biannual sermon Offering moment	Biannual sermon Offering moment

New	Stewardship Education New members' class	Stewardship Education New members' class	New members' class Biannual sermon Offering moment	New members' class Biannual sermon Offering moment
Immature	Stewardship Education Biannual sermon	Stewardship Education Biannual sermon	Leader giving standard Biannual sermon	Leader giving standard Biannual sermon
Maturing	Stewardship Education	Stewardship Education	Vision Offering moment Vision Partners Appreciation Vision meetings Generosity champion	Vision Offering moment Vision Partners Appreciation Vision meetings Generosity champion

As you can see from the table above, most of the generosity focus is on the solid maturing and surplus maturing groups. While many pastors make the mistake of ignoring the discipleship of people who already give significantly (successful maturing and surplus maturing groups), I will encourage you to make these groups your biggest focus. The reason is that as these groups go, so goes the culture of your church. If they are strong, they will lift others. The other reason is that they have financial resources.

FOCUS ON THE GIVER, NOT THE GIFT

You can spend a whole lot of effort talking about tithing and make only a small impact on your budget or spend a little effort taking to tithers about generosity and have a significant impact on your budget. This is the easiest and most impactful way to increase financial resources to reach your vision.

I was talking to a guy who makes about $400,000 annually and gives $40,000 in tithes to his church. He shared with me that he also gave another $40,000 to several nonprofit organizations. When I asked why he didn't give more to his church, he said, "They never asked for more. I thought all they wanted and needed was my tithe." There is nothing wrong with Christians being generous outside of the church, but this guy would have happily given more toward God's work via his local church if he had been discipled more in the area of generosity.

When you are overly focused on tithing, you are saying to this guy, "You've done enough. We don't need any more of your money." You rob this guy of fulfilling his God-given purpose of giving generously toward God's work.

The successful and surplus maturing groups are the best to pastor because they are already with you and support you. This doesn't mean you ignore those who do not have financial resources. It only means you have different tactics to reach the different people in your church.

I will spend the remaining chapters explaining the ten strategies for developing a generous church in detail.

CHAPTER 5

Communicate a Compelling Vision

Churches are competing with secular and Christian nonprofit organizations for their members' charitable dollars. Many times, churches lose out to organizations that do a better job communicating their charitable need. Nonprofit organizations such as colleges and hospitals are experts at attracting donors. They don't point to leaking roofs or rising cost of utilities. They connect donors to the people's lives they will impact. Even though they may be raising funds to build a new building, they paint a picture of how donations will save little Becky Sue's life. Churches have the most compelling cause ever—to help everyone we know have a personal relationship with God through Jesus. There is no more worthwhile cause. But we do a poor job communicating it, which limits our ability to raise the funds needed to carry out this vision. Vision takes money.

> "Write down the revelation and make it plain on tablets so that a herald may run with it" (Habakkuk 2:2 NIV).

The word "plain" means simple—easy to understand, deal with, or use. The vision needs to be communicated in a way that makes it easy enough for people to easily get involved and run with it. Simple also means manageable, and sometimes simple means less. God loves to simplify things. Jesus simplified how we should live by saying "love God and love others."

One of the lead pastor's goals should be to better communicate a compelling church vision.

A vision is a picture of a preferable future.

> "Where there is no vision, the people perish" (Proverbs 29:18 King James Version).

When we don't fully understand our purpose, we drift into existing in a life less than what God called us to live. One of the biggest reasons that churches don't grow is an unclear vision. They typically have something written down and may have it memorized, but most church members do not really know what they are trying to accomplish.

I met with a pastor who shared a very compelling vision for the church. Afterward, I met individually with all of his key staff leaders and asked them what they believed to be the vision of the church. Surprisingly, they all gave me different answers. It was clear that the pastor had a vision from God that would truly impact God's kingdom, but because it was not clearly communicated, the church was making very little progress toward making the vision a reality. When we have a clear and compelling vision, there is no limit to what we can do.

God has given each church the people and resources it needs to carry out the vision He called it to do. I have learned that people give to vision. Generous people desperately desire to invest in a big cause. When they do not understand where the church is headed, they choose to give to other organizations.

Many churches go through life out of breath because they are in so many activities, many of which do not contribute to their purpose.

In order for the church to accomplish its vision, it must eliminate events, activities, and relationships that don't contribute to who they are and what they are about. The church must know who they are and where they fit into the body of Christ. No church can do everything. Each must pick its cause and stick to it. You have to put every idea, program, and budget request through the filter of your vision or purpose.

Ask, "How does this line up with the vision God has for us?" It could be a great activity, but if it doesn't line up with the vision God has for us, then we can't do it. Stick to your vision and don't try to be someone else. If you keep His vision in front of you, keep your hope in Him, and stay faithful and accountable, you will accomplish exactly what God meant for you to do.

Lead pastors should take time each year to share the vision for the upcoming year and invite the congregation

TRAVIS MOODY

to give toward an annual "vision" offering. The vision should consist of five to seven key initiatives and include the estimated cost to fund each initiative.

These initiatives should be whatever vision God has for your church. However, it is critical that they are compelling and large enough to inspire high-capacity givers to get involved in funding. The total cost of vision initiatives should be in the range of 20–35 percent of the annual budget. If the amount needed for the vision is too small, those who could give large amounts begin to think that their resources are not needed.

Examples of key initiatives are as follows:

- Launch a new mobile campus in downtown (equipment, advertising, and launch cost)—$510,000.
- Expand children's area in order to accommodate more students—$160,000.
- Purchase and renovate bus for after-school literacy program—$50,000.
- Create and fully equip national disaster readiness team—$200,000.
- Provide financial support to ministry partners in Israel that are committed to cultivating Messiah-centered relationships that bless the inhabitants of Israel—$100,000.

CHAPTER 6

Have an Effective Offering Moment During Weekend Services

The offering moment is an excellent opportunity to connect people with the church vision. It reminds them of how their financial sacrifices are impacting people for Christ. At the Life Church, we put emphasis on generosity. The offering moment includes these key points:

- **Communicate giving to "changed lives" through effective storytelling**. Typically, people aren't inspired to give to fix the roof or replace the carpet. People are inspired by having a positive impact on the lives of others. Effective storytelling helps people to connect their giving to changing lives. To help people further make the connection, we often share brief videos during the offering moment showing how some person's life has been impacted by our church. This gives people a face to the impact of their generosity.

- **Do not pressure or guilt people into giving.** It is more than okay to set an expectation of members to give, but do not put pressure on people to give. I encourage this for two reasons. First, it would not be effective. Eventually, members would begin to distrust you and hold back from being generous, knowing the pressure will soon come. Second, I don't recommend putting pressure on people to give because it's unbiblical. In 2 Corinthians 9:7, it says, "Each one should give what he has decided in his heart to give, not reluctantly or under pressure for God loves a cheerful giver!" God doesn't want people giving out of obligation any more than He would want us to pray or go to church out of obligation. He cares more about our heart.

- **Encourage giving above the tithe (i.e., generosity).** There needs to be more focus on generosity than there is on tithing. Words that reflect generosity are offering, generous, and giving. I encourage pastors to change their language during the offering moment. A good rule of thumb is to use a five-to-one ratio. For every time you use the word *tithe*, use words like *generosity*, *offering*, and *giving* five times or more.

- **Provide various, easy, and clearly communicated giving options.** These days, people handle money in so many different ways that were not available several years ago. In the past, putting money in the collection plate at church was the only way to give. Fewer people carry cash or write checks. Many people prefer to give online or through their mobile phone. We currently receive about 70 percent of our giving electronically. Churches have to adapt to how people handle money. Make giving options easy, clear, relatable, user friendly, and safe. These options should be clearly communicated so all givers know how to give.

CHAPTER 7

Preach on Finances

E very church should preach on money at least twice a year. This needs to be a clear life-giving message to encourage people to handle money God's way. There are so many people who do not understand God's way of handling money and therefore are not flourishing in their finances.

I have this saying that I use to help pastors teach the subject of money in church: "no wimping and no pimping." I find that many churches operate at these two extremes when it comes to teaching on money in church.

Wimping is when churches avoid dealing with the subject of money to avoid making people feel uncomfortable. When they do this, they miss out on helping people in a real tangible way.

Experts report 80 percent of Americans worry about money all the time (Tracy, *Maximum Achievement*, 28). Conflict over money is one of the top causes of divorce. Even though we live in one of the wealthiest countries in the world, we are a society where many of us are living paycheck to paycheck and praying to God we don't lose our jobs because we don't know how we would make it a week without our income.

The church has an obligation to speak on the subject of money in a clear and bold way to help people live a flourishing life.

At the other extreme are churches who are pimping their congregations by abusing and misrepresenting biblical financial messages for selfish gain or out of lack of knowledge.

These churches teach what many call prosperity gospel. They teach if you give to God, then you will receive more money back. This type of teaching is flawed, although scriptures support that when we give sacrificially to God with our financial resources, our lives are blessed in return (Proverbs 11:25 NIV). This includes financial blessings. However, it doesn't mean you will necessarily have financial wealth.

This is also the wrong motivation. We don't give to get. We give out of a desire to do everything we can to impact our world for Christ.

Many people have been wounded in the area of money by the church. They have felt guilt and condemnation to give. They have seen church leaders misuse church funds and lead with the wrong motives. This further feeds the enemy's lies that all the church wants is your money.

Although it is a small minority of clergy who lead this way, the small minority seem to get the biggest attention, thus making all ministry leaders look bad. This is a battle we will continue to face, but we can't shy away from teaching money in church because of it.

Pastors can't allow past hurts to keep them from boldly teaching money messages. People need to hear biblical truths concerning money, and they need to hear it from their pastor.

We have to connect financial decisions to spiritual decisions. The attitude we should take is something I heard Andy Stanley say, "We talk about money not because of what we want *from* you but because of what we want *for* you." We teach on money because we want every follower of Jesus to experience the freedom that comes with living a generous life toward God.

What to Teach

Be creative with teaching finances, but generally encourage people to do these three things:

1. Tithe consistently
2. Manage responsibly
3. Build a generous spirit

Tithe Consistently

Most Christians are familiar with the term tithe but may not understand what it really means. The term tithe literally means "a tenth part," just like the word half means 50 percent or a quarter means 25 percent.

The definition of tithing most often used is bringing the first 10 percent of my gross income to God through my local church. Tithing gives a vision for giving systematically. It provides a clear benchmark for action.

Those who are serious about living for God make Him the number one priority in every area of their lives. It's easy to say God is first priority, but actual spending choices reveal our true priorities. When God is truly first priority, it is reflected in our finances.

The goal when teaching on the subject of tithing is to connect financial decisions to spiritual decisions. It is not about what the church wants from members but about what the church wants for members. The objective is to help free people from the bondage that the love of money can have on them and move them into a closer relationship with Christ. Don't subscribe to the "give to get" mentality. This is the wrong attitude for giving.

The truth is everything belongs to God, not just 10 percent but 100 percent. Tithing is a tangible way to show God honor, love, and trust.

Money-Back Guarantee

In Malachi 3:10 (NIV), God says, "Test me in this … and see if I will not throw open the floodgates of heaven and pour out so much blessing that there will not be room enough to store it."

Encourage your church to test God by offering a ninety-day tithe challenge with a money-back guarantee.

Don't subscribe to a "give to get" mentality. That mentality says, "If you give money, God will give you back more money." As mentioned earlier, giving to get is the wrong attitude. Nevertheless, it is absolutely true that God blesses those who are generous toward the things of God. That truth should give you great confidence that God will do what He said He would do.

In this challenge, invite those in your church who are not tithing to try tithing for ninety days. Explain that if at the end of the ninety days, they don't feel God has kept up His end of the deal, the church will give their tithes back from the ninety-day period.

Provide a way for people to let you know they are committing to the challenge. This could be a physical commitment card or online form. Send this group weekly emails to encourage them on their journey and provide stewardship classes to help them in practical ways.

The table below shows results from a tithe challenge I was a part of recently.

Ninety-Day Tithe Challenge Giving Summary

Type	Number	Percent
New givers	171	38%
Sporadic givers	151	33%
Regular but not tithing	57	13%
Tithing givers	72	16%

Overall Giving

In the challenge reported above, 451 out of 2,470 giving units responded (18 percent of church). You can typically expect around 10 percent of the church attenders to take the challenge each time it is offered. Giving for the challengers increased by $22,422 or 25 percent over the previous month. That equals $269,064 annually. Having a regular tithe challenge is a way to consistently develop new and sporadic givers into tithers.

A surprising benefit of the challenge is that it is a way of identifying new Vision Partners. In the challenge example above, forty-one of the seventy-two giving units who were already tithing self-identified as potential new Vision Partners.

Several pastors have expressed concerns to me over having a money-back guarantee. They envision having to give people their money back. It's true that it's a risk, but it's a very small risk. Occasionally, someone will ask for their tithe back, but it's very rare. In the years I have been a part of this challenge, I've seen thousands of families take the challenge, yet out of those thousands of families, only once or twice a year does anyone ever ask for their money back. In each of those cases, the amount has been less than $1,000. When the annual increase is over $200,000, it's more than worth the risk of repaying a couple thousand dollars a year.

Manage Responsibly

The second thing to teach is how to manage responsibly. It would be irresponsible for us as leaders to tell people to give 10 percent of their income and not teach them how to live on the 90 percent that's remaining.

Please refer to my first book, *Financial Breakthrough, God's Plan for Getting out of Debt*, as a resource for helping people understand how to manage finances well. In it, I share details of how my wife and I were able to pay off more than $100,000 in personal debt over just three years. Here are five pieces of practical financial advice I like to give:

1. Get the facts about your financial situation.

Think of yourself as a corporation and God as an investor. Then ask yourself, would God invest in you? God is an investor in our lives, and He's going to have the same questions any good investor would have:

- What's your income?
- What are your operating expenses?
- What's your profit margin?
- What is your debt ratio?

There are so many of us who cannot answer these questions. This is how most of us sound to God. "Well, I don't know exactly how much I earn or where I spend it. I'm certainly not making a profit. I don't know how much debt I have, but I know it's a lot. I just know I don't have enough money, so will you give me more?"

None of us would invest in a company like this, so why would God invest in a person knowing that there is no return on His investment? Jesus said, "Whoever can be trusted with very little can also be trusted with much, and whoever is dishonest with very little will also be dishonest with much. So if you have not been trustworthy in handling worldly wealth, who will trust you with true riches?" (Luke 16:10–11 NIV). We have to be honest with ourselves and ask, "Would God buy my stock?"

Getting the facts about our financial situation starts with these four questions:

- How much do I earn (e.g., gross not just net)?
- How much and where do I spend?
- How much do I owe?
- How much do I own?

The answers to these questions will help you develop a budget or spending plan. You can't really make good financial decisions without answering these questions.

2. Create an emergency fund with at least $1,000.

Even before paying off debt, we suggest you put away $1,000 for emergencies. Things will happen. If you don't have money set aside for emergencies, you cannot break the debt cycle. Now an emergency is not a pair of shoes that is on sale or finding a new suit for graduation. I recommend starting with at least $1,000 because in the United States, most emergencies cost about $1,000. Replacing a refrigerator or repairing a car or A/C unit cost about $1,000. Most people have $1,000 deductibles on cars and homes. Most unexpected medical emergencies can be taken care of for $1,000.

3. Establish a spending plan.

Some people don't like budgets because they believe it takes away their freedom, but budgets actually provide freedom. There was a group of kids playing on a playground next to a busy street. Some parents stopped letting their kids play there because of the danger from the cars. Then one day, the city put up a fence. Now the kids had the freedom to play right up to the fence. The fence did not limit them; it only protected them and provided freedom to play and have fun without the worry of danger. That's what a budget does for us. It clearly sets our safety boundaries. It says to us, "As long as you play on this side of the fence, you are safe." The problem with some of us is that we jump the fence and play in the busy freeway and then wonder why we got hit by a semi. Budgeting is a critical step in becoming financially free.

A budget or spending plan is an itemized summary of projected income and expenses. It's important because it simplifies your spending decisions and helps you achieve your financial goals. Key elements of a budget or spending plan are that it must …

- be written
- use categories, such as groceries, rent, gas, utilities, and so on
- be balanced (i.e., budgeted expenses must be less than budgeted income)
- be realistic ($0 for entertainment is not realistic)
- include all expected income and expenses

Luke 14:28 (NIV) says, "Suppose one of you wants to build a tower. Won't you first sit down and estimate the cost to see if you have enough money to complete it?"

Jesus reminds us that it is wise to start with a plan or budget before beginning to spend. A budget helps you plan how you will spend money.

4. Purchase a home and car you can afford.

Ninety percent of the financial problems are caused by two decisions—the choice of a home and of an automobile. Typically, if we can get these two decisions right, we are usually okay financially. We get into trouble when we see how God blessed someone else and get anxious to see progress in our own lives.

God doesn't mind us having nice things. In fact, He loves to bless us with nice homes and cars. He just wants us to wait for Him to provide it and not overextend ourselves.

When it comes to making home and car-purchasing decisions, I think it's smart to stick to these two basic guidelines.

- No more than 20 percent of gross income on mortgage or rent.
- No more than 7 percent of gross income on car financing.

Obviously, it would be best to pay cash for a car, but realistically, not everyone will have resources for that option. I should also note that I do not recommend financing a car for more than sixty months at current interest rates. If interest rates increase, I typically reduce the suggested max financing to thirty-six or forty-eight months. These are just guidelines and not to be used as a religious law. I have formed these after coaching so many people over the years and observing those who live on a balanced budget. I found that following these guidelines provides the best environment to live on a balanced budget and be financially free.

5. Create and execute a plan to eliminate debt.

Although debt may help people have all the luxuries of life, the burden of debt then controls their lifestyle. They become enslaved to their financial situation. It is like the bumper sticker that reads, "I owe, I owe, so off to work I go." Although the Bible doesn't say debt is a sin, it definitely discourages the use of debt. Proverbs 22:7 (NIV) says, "The rich rule over the poor, and the borrower is slave to the lender."

Today, many people live in financial chaos. Too often, people are living paycheck to paycheck and using one credit card to pay the minimum on another credit card. Everything looks fine to those on the outside, but the reality is excessive debt and no real wealth. Debt wears people down not only financially but also spiritually, emotionally, and physically. This is certainly not the financial position God wants for His people.

6. Save 10 percent for the future.

The wise have wealth and luxury, but fools spend whatever they get (Proverbs 21:20 NLT).

God gives a certain amount to spend today plus some to put away for the future. We may not know what our financial needs are in the future, but God does. It is foolish for us to spend all we have today and not store away any for the future.

The Bible doesn't suggest a certain amount, but I agree with many other experts and suggest saving at least 10 percent of your gross income.

If your company has a 401k program, you should take advantage of that. Especially if they offer a match, you should invest up to the company match.

Build a Generous Spirit

The third principle to teach is to build a generous spirit. As I mentioned earlier, tithing is not the goal. Generosity is the goal.

One of the scriptures most often quoted in the Bible that deals with the subject of giving is Malachi 3:8 (NKJV). In fact, most of us have heard this verse so much that we know it by heart.

"Will a man rob God? Yet you have robbed Me! But you say, 'In what way have we robbed You?' In tithes and offerings."

This is one of the few scriptures that makes me cringe when I hear it in church. I know that can't be good for a stewardship pastor. It's not because it's not truth or I didn't believe it but because it's so often abused or misunderstood.

Somehow when most of us read this scripture, we miss what I think is the key word in this scripture. This scripture says we "rob God in tithes and offering." That word "and" is a conjunction, meaning both of these are important. This scripture is addressing both tithes *and* offerings. Both tithes and offerings bring honor to God because both represent what God did for us through Jesus Christ.

Christ was both a tithe and an offering. When God considered how He would restore His people, He chose to send His best. He never considered sending someone else. He didn't say, "Why don't I send an angel like Gabriel or Michael?" No. He didn't hesitate to send His son, Jesus, as a tithe. Jesus also served as God's offering as He willingly sacrificed His life for our sins on the cross.

Tithing is not generosity. It's only when we give offerings that we begin a lifestyle of generosity. So what's the difference between a tithe and an offering?

Remember a tithe is bringing the first tenth of my income to God through my local church. The offering is symbolic of the sacrifice of Jesus Christ. The animals used in biblical offerings had to be "without defect" to be acceptable to God (Leviticus 1:3 NIV). In the same way, Jesus was "a lamb without blemish or defect" (1 Peter 1:19 NIV), an acceptable gift for our sins.

The Bible uses the words offering and sacrifice interchangeably. An offering is something given or sacrificed by choice. It is any gift given over and above the tithe. Where a tithe amount was determined, the amount of an offering is determined by the giver.

So many Christians don't understand the word offering. It's not a word that we use often in everyday life. A member told me once, "Well, I can't tithe, but I can give an offering." Since an offering is anything I give in addition to my tithe, it's impossible to give an offering without also giving a tithe.

Therefore, if a person is not at least tithing, then they by default rob God of offerings as well. For example, if you had $120 in your purse, and a person stole $100 out of your purse but left a twenty, you would not say that person offered you twenty. No—that person robbed you of $100!

I think the most important and most overlooked word of Malachi 3:8 is the word offering. The offering gets to the heart of building a generous spirit. The term offering wasn't such a big deal to me until one day I read a scripture that messed me up. Since I struggle with it, you are going to have to struggle with it too.

The scripture was Isaiah 52:14 (NIV).

Just as there were many who were appalled at him—his appearance was so disfigured beyond that of any human being and his form marred beyond human likeness.

Isaiah is prophesying about Jesus's crucifixion. Most of us have this image of Jesus quietly suffering on the cross, but this paints a different picture.

The truth is that Jesus was beaten so badly He did not look like a human being. I could not believe what I was reading and asked myself, "How does this even happen?" As I continued to study, this is what I found out.

- He was beaten by the high priest (Matthew 26:68).
- Pilate's soldiers beat him with a staff on the head again and again (Matthew 27:30).
- Then Jesus was flogged (Mark 15:15).

In the Roman Empire, flogging was often used as a prelude to crucifixion. They used whips with small pieces of metal or bone at the tips to cause disfigurement and serious trauma. The good floggers would rip pieces of flesh from the body or cause the loss of an eye. These floggers were likely the best.

According to the Jewish law, the lashes could not exceed thirty-nine, but these were Roman soldiers who didn't stick to Jewish culture. Jesus was beaten and disfigured to the point they couldn't even tell if he was a human. Eyes closed. Flesh and hair ripped from his skin. Private parts exposed. Then He was nailed to a cross that He couldn't even carry the weight of.

I was okay when I had this picture of Jesus quietly suffering on the cross, but this image messed me up. "Disfigured beyond human likeness."

Yet the worst part was not the physical pain. The worst part was that, for the first time, He felt separated from God.

When Jesus took on my sin, for the first time he felt what we feel when we sin—separated from God. That's what sin does. He felt the isolation, loneliness, depression, guilt, shame, and everything else that comes along with feeling separated from God. He had never experienced this before. Jesus cried out, "My God, my God, why have you forsaken me?" (Matthew 27:46 NIV).

The only thing that kept Him on that cross is that He looked out in the future and saw my face. He loved me so much He couldn't stand to live without me.

The difference in the tithe and the offering is that the offering is a choice. We don't get to choose our tithe. It belongs to God. But the offering is ours to choose.

Jesus chose to give Himself as an offering. He chose to die for my sins, so I could live with Him forever in heaven.

He agonized over the decision the night before. He prayed to God to ask if there was some other way, but ultimately Jesus said, "Not my will but your will be done." Sacrifice is always a choice.

I will never understand why Jesus made that choice for me and why He loved me so much. But He did. He did this for me.

Scripture says we should give in proportion to the way God has blessed us (Deuteronomy 16:17). I don't know how to respond to that kind of love. I do know one thing. I can't read or hear this scripture ever again without seeing this image of Christ. It's the offering that stands out to me.

I don't share this message to condemn people. Condemnation doesn't come from God. That's the trick of the enemy. I share so people will know how much Jesus loves them and to inspire them to live a life of gratitude to Him for what He did for us.

Isaiah foretells what Jesus did for us that day on the cross in Isaiah 53:5 (NIV): "But he was pierced for our transgressions, he was crushed for our iniquities; the punishment that brought us peace was on him, and by his wounds we are healed."

Living a lifestyle of generosity is our response to what Jesus did for us. It allows us to experience the peace and freedom that comes from giving our whole life as an offering and sacrifice to God.

CHAPTER 8

Invite Tithers to Become Generous Givers (Vision Partners)

The easiest and most impactful way to increase church giving is to invite those who are already tithing to become above the tithe givers or what I call generous givers or Vision Partners.

Prior to sharing the annual vision with the church, pastors should plan an event to share the vision first with Vision Partners. It is important to share with them so that they feel they are being kept in the loop concerning the direction of the church. Plan this annual Vision Partner evening or weekend retreat at a nice high-end hotel or event center.

This is not an event to ask for a certain amount. Instead, Vision Partners are encouraged to spend time with

God to determine how He would want them to commit toward the vision. There is no pressure, and there are no gimmicks. They should not feel guilt, shame, pressure, or condemnation when it comes to their level of giving. Simply share openly and clearly the vision God has given and how much it will cost. Allow God to lead people to give however He sees fit.

The vision offering received is typically around an additional 20 percent of the annual budget, and 70 percent of the vision offering comes from Vision Partners. When I joined the Life Church staff, 3.5 percent of our giving units were Vision Partners. Over the next five years, that number increased over fivefold to more than 18 percent.

While others are complaining about how hard it is to be forced to ride the bike with training wheels, Vision Partners have learned to ride the bike of generosity freely and cheerfully. They feel privileged to have the opportunity to partner with God to fund His vision. They have learned that life is only truly lived when you are giving it away to others. They are enjoying the journey of growing in the area of living a generous life.

Vision Partners have the call and the financial resources to fund God's work on earth. You don't have to seek out generous people. They will find you. You just need to know how to listen when they speak with their giving.

If I asked a pastor who their most generous person is, they immediately think about who seemingly has the highest-paying job or business. This person may not be generous at all. Generous people …

- give a significant percentage of their income

sport package so he could haul his toys around. John was excited about beginning his new life with Amy, his soon-to-be bride. When she saw the black velvet-covered box, it took her breath away. But when she opened it, her reaction changed. She tried not to seem disappointed, but when she found out John had spent only $250 on the ring, she was devastated. It was not that she was materialistic, but she cried and asked if he really loved her. John responded, "The amount of the ring doesn't matter anyway. After all, it's the heart that counts" (Anderson, *Plastic Donuts*, 27–28).

A lot of Christians have this same opinion: "The amount doesn't matter … God knows my heart." While the heart is crucial, the amount does matter. In fact, it's the amount that engages the heart. Jesus said, "For where your treasure is, there your heart will be also" (Matthew 6:21 NIV). Wherever we spend money, our hearts have to follow.

We all have amounts that matter to us, such as our home mortgage, car payments, and so on. Because these amounts matter to us, we are diligent to set aside the money for these items.

Our giving to God should be no different. We should give gifts to God that cost us something and that we value. This will require us to live counterculturally and have a Christ-centered, eternal perspective.

When a man wanted to give King David what he needed to give an offering to God, David replied, "No, I insist on paying you for it. I will not sacrifice to the Lord my God burnt offerings that cost me nothing" (2 Samuel 24:24 NIV). An offering always causes us to sacrifice something we value. We sacrifice something we value for something we value more.

God accepts our gifts when we give gifts that matter to us. When we sacrifice things of this world to invest in things that matter to Him, scripture says, "It is like a pleasing aroma to God" (Exodus 29:18 NIV). If it matters to us, then it matters to God. If it doesn't matter to us, then it will not matter to God.

CHAPTER 9

Provide Giver Appreciation and Follow-Up

I learned this vital lesson from my friend Larry Lloyd. He encouraged me to get in the habit of sending thank-you notes to givers. Larry has founded and led several successful nonprofits, and he shared with me how people in the nonprofit world recognize the importance of appreciating people for their giving. We would be wise to learn this same lesson in the church world.

Some pastors have a hard problem with thanking people for doing what they perceive is their Christian duty. But appreciating people is a way to help people understand and participate in the vision of the church. It is a positive reinforcement of the behavior we want.

One of the most influential of American psychologists, B. F. Skinner concluded, "Behavior which is reinforced tends to be repeated (i.e., strengthened); behavior which is not reinforced tends to die out—or be extinguished (i.e., weakened)." When we appreciate people for giving in church, we strengthen generosity in our church.

Here are a couple practical opportunities to say thank you:

- **First-time gifts**. We send a thank-you note to every first-time giver. This is a form letter from our pastor thanking the person for their gift. We want them to know that we noticed and that their gift matters to us and to God. We run this report and send these notes weekly.

- **Special large ($1,000 or more) gifts**. We send a handwritten thank-you note to any unique gifts over $1,000. These are special gifts over $1,000. For instance, if a person gives $1,000 each month, then they would not receive a thank-you note each month. They would receive it only the first month. For most of those who receive this thank you, it's the first time they have ever been thanked for giving to their church. Because of that, it means a lot to them that their church appreciates their generosity.

  Running this report weekly is critical in identifying potential Vision Partners. The best way to identify those with the gift of giving is by their actions. Generous people love to give. They can't help it. That's how God wired them, and that's why God gave them the financial resources. Our job is to help disciple them in the way that God created them. If we don't, then other nonprofit organizations will, and their spiritual gift of giving goes to benefit colleges, hospitals, and other nonprofits. There's nothing wrong with those things. They all have great causes, but there is no cause greater than God's. We have to be as good at fundraising as other nonprofits.

If a person can write a one-time check for $1,000, you best believe they can write a lot more. For that reason, I add these givers to a potential Vision Partner list. I monitor the giving of those on this list and invite them to Vision Partner events. It's usually not long before they choose to become Vision Partners.

CHAPTER 10

Have Intentional Vision Partner Meetings

B eing intentional about meeting with high-capacity givers is critical to building a generous church culture. I encourage fifteen to twenty-five touches throughout the year. A touch could be a phone call, text, email, or one-on-one meeting. A benefit of having regular touches throughout the year is that it takes away the feeling that you are just meeting with them when it's time for the annual giving pledge. The most effective touch is having a one-on-one meeting for coffee or lunch. I personally spend about 60 percent of my time meeting with high-capacity givers. I estimate that I have had over a thousand of these meetings as stewardship pastor at the Life Church. Not once have I met with someone to ask for money. There are five objectives for these meetings.

1. **Relationship building**. The best thing we can do to for high-capacity givers is be a pastor to them. Just because they have money doesn't mean they do not have issues. We meet with them to build a relationship so that we can effectively pastor them. In order for them to sustain generosity at a high level, they need to be living overall healthy lives. Having a trusted relationship with them opens the door for me to speak into their lives. It provides the opportunity for me to ask, "How are you doing?" I have helped people with marriage issues, spiritual struggles, health concerns, parenting issues, financial decisions, and more. This gives us a chance to love on them and be a pastor for them.

2. **Discuss vision activities**. I usually spend a few minutes sharing a brief update on vision activities and answering any questions they may have concerning these activities.

3. **Develop/promote/connect business leaders**. Many of the high-capacity givers are business people. I usually ask how their business is going and see if there are people we know that we can help connect them with for business or their personal development. There have been many occasions where I have been able to recommend another business to partner with or another Vision Partner

to hire for a particular job. When we can connect high-capacity givers to each other, everyone wins.

4. **Give appreciation**. I always take the opportunity to thank and appreciate Vision Partners for their giving. This lets them know we don't take for granted that they have committed to being a generous giver at our church. I make sure this doesn't feel like a backhanded way of asking for more money. I purposely stay away from asking for money.

5. **Discipleship**. I always ask something like, "What's your next step at church?" This gives me a chance to disciple them and help move their spiritual life forward. I'm listening for unresolved spiritual issues or possible next steps. It's critical that your church has clearly identified spiritual steps. Seek to understand where they are. Don't be judgmental or critical, but in a life-giving way, encourage them to take their next step spiritually.

CHAPTER 11

Hold Leaders Accountable to a Giving Standard

As I mentioned earlier, you can't have people who aren't financial disciples become part of the leadership. Having a clear giving standard helps to establish a generous culture. When generosity begins with leaders, it saturates the culture. It also prevents spiritually immature people from infiltrating higher levels of leadership.

We want people to imitate leaders, so it's important to hold leaders to a giving standard. You can't recreate what you are not. Jesus taught this concept in Luke 6:39–40.

He also told them this parable: "Can the blind lead the blind? Will they not both fall into a pit? The student is not above the teacher, but everyone who is fully trained will be like their teacher" (Luke 6:39–40 NIV).

A generous church must start with a full internal and external commitment of the senior leader to personally live out stewardship and publicly support the ministry. This sets the tone for the entire church. Second, make it a requirement for leaders to at least tithe in order to serve in a leadership capacity—any staff or lay leader position that entails leading others. This also means that someone has to check giving records for leaders.

It's important to note that tithing is an expectation of every member, but the only time we hold people to the standard is when they opt to step into leadership.

I feel so strongly about this that even if the Bible had not mentioned tithing, I would still consider it an expectation for leaders. It's a good culture-setting expectation. It is similar to how most pastors would expect good leaders to attend church consistently.

As stewardship pastor, one of my responsibilities is to review giving records for anyone applying to attend a leadership class. It's best to address any issues early in the process. It provides a clear standard for new leaders.

I also check giving records for all staff and current leaders at least quarterly. Because we address issues early in the process, we rarely have an issue with leaders not tithing. When we do, we quickly meet with the individual to discuss their giving. This provides opportunity to disciple leaders.

On one of these occasions, we found that one of our leaders had stopped tithing. I met with him to discuss it. It turns out he and his wife were having some marriage and financial issues. We were able to meet with them both to provide counseling and help them create a financial plan. We removed him from leadership while he was working through these issues. It wasn't long before they had worked through the issues and we were able to reinstate him back into his leadership position. This family was very grateful that we had helped them work through a difficult situation. It wasn't about the money. It was about loving them enough to hold them accountable. We never do this in a blaming or threatening way. We always approach these conversations with the attitude of how do we help our brother or sister.

Holding leaders to a clear giving standard helps to build a highly committed and engaged leadership culture.

CHAPTER 12

Offer Regular Stewardship Education and Coaching

Stewardship classes must be relevant and engaging. They must also have a biblically centered curriculum. There are many resources out there, such as Crown Financial, Dave Ramsey, and Compass. All of them are great. We have had success with using them all at different points in our ministry. It really just depends on which fits best with your church.

Regardless of what curriculum you use, it's critical that you have gifted and passionate teaching.

It's important that you promote money classes the right way. If you promote it to the church as a class to help people in financial need or dealing with a lot of debt, then people will not come. They will be too embarrassed.

Promote it with the stable or surplus person in mind. Call the financial workshop something like Winning in Your Finances. Explain this is for anyone and not just for the ones in hard financial situations. This allows you to reach a diverse group financially.

Here are some different teaching options to provide at your church:

- **Seven-week financial workshop**. My flagship teaching solution is a seven-week workshop. I created a curriculum that combines money coaching and a biblical financial study. Each week, there is a different topic covered, with practical assignments like tracking your spending, listing debts, or creating an estimated budget. Each person is assigned a money coach to answer questions and help them complete their weekly assignments. I found this to be the most effective way to impact people's lives. It combines spiritual lessons, practical assignments, coaching, and accountability.

- **Financial seminars**. Seminars are one-day events that cover the same material I teach in our seven-week workshop in one full day. It's not as effective as the workshop, but it attracts those who are less willing to commit to seven weeks.

  Note: I encourage you to charge a minimal fee for workshops and seminars. Having a fee does three things.

  1. It covers the cost of materials and refreshments.

2. It helps with having an accurate count for class participation so you can plan appropriately.

3. It gives participants some skin in the game. I learned the hard way that sometimes when classes are provided for free, people don't value them. It doesn't matter to them if they come or not because it didn't cost them anything. When they pay thirty dollars, it gives them more commitment to attend and complete the class. In cases where people say that they cannot afford the fee, require that they write a check for the registration amount with the agreement that if they complete the class, you will return the check, but if they do not complete the class, you will cash the check. This takes away their excuse and motivates them to complete the class.

- **Financial small group study**. Offer curriculum for small group studies such as Crown, Compass, or Financial Peace.

- **Topical workshops**. Throughout the year, offer standalone classes to help people in a particular area, such as the following:
  - buying a car
  - understanding your 401(k)
  - finding a job
  - buying a home
  - estate planning
  - paying off student loans

- funding college
- investing for the everyday millionaire

These classes can go in more detail on a topic than you could cover in the seven-week workshop. Try to cover the most relevant topics that most people have questions about.

- **One-on-one money coaching**. Create a team of money coaches to help people create a budget and make critical money decisions. The majority of people who seek money coaches have decided to get on a budget but do not know where to start. Direct those who seek money coaching to attend a workshop or small group study. This is a better use of your coaches' time. Make it a requirement for anyone who requests benevolence or financial assistance from the church to meet with a money coach. This deters those who are not really in need and allows you to focus on those who really need help. Even within this group, most of the benevolence requests are handled with budget adjustments and not with providing financial assistance from the church. Oftentimes, financial needs can be dealt with by making small adjustments such as eliminating cable television and spending less on dining out and entertainment. It may not be what people want to hear, but having coaches who can go through the details of people's financial lives is critical in helping people grow in the area of their finances.

CHAPTER 13

Teach Generous Giving in New Members' Class

You will also need to teach it early so new members hear it as they join church. It is important for members to hear a consistent money message at the beginning as well as throughout their journey in church.

The messages they need to hear are as follows:

- A clear definition that tithing is consistently giving 10 percent of their gross income to God through their local church.
- Tithing is a baby step. The goal is generosity.
- Tithing is an expectation of every member.
- Vision Partners are people who feel called to give significantly to resource God's work.

CHAPTER 14

Assign a Generous Church Champion/Leader

A critical pillar to your success in building a generous church is finding and empowering a passionate and capable leader, either staff or nonstaff. Here is my job description at the Life Church:

The stewardship and generosity pastor is dedicated to developing a culture of generosity at the Life Church. The stewardship and generosity pastor will provide spiritual leadership, vision, and direction for the stewardship and generosity ministry, an integrated stewardship ministry that includes Vision Partners ministry, stewardship education and training, business ministry, and money coaching. All activities will be focused toward fulfilling the ministry mission of equipping people to experience the joy of living by biblical financial principles. The stewardship and generosity pastor is responsible for recruiting, training, and developing others in the stewardship and generosity ministry.

Below are some qualifications and responsibilities to consider in the stewardship and generosity champion:

1. Works in partnership with the senior pastor and leadership team to establish strategic direction for the ministry
2. Good representative of the church
3. Understands and models generous giving
4. Passionate about growing others in the area of generosity
5. Credibility with high-capacity people
6. Not intimidated by wealthy people, strong egos, or influencers
7. Long-term committed history to senior pastor and church
8. Engaged in church's vision
9. Ability to analyze giving data and reports (i.e., top-givers report and pledge reports)
10. Initiates activities that build personal relationships with Vision Partners and potential Vision Partners
11. Coordinates and tracks relationship-building and appreciation activities with senior pastor and leadership team
12. Coordinates Vision Partner events (brunch, dinner, etc.)
13. Communicates regularly by email to Vision Partners (weekly devotionals, quarterly reports, welcome emails, event invitations, etc.)

14. Previous executive business experience valuable
15. Can connect people with appropriate ministry resources (money coaching, marriage counseling, pastoral counseling, etc.) or business partnerships
16. Able to recruit, train, and develop other ministry leaders from Vision Partners

CHAPTER 15

Generosity Metrics

I t's important to have the right metrics. Building a culture of generosity is not a quick fix. It's a long-term commitment. Over time, you should see an increase in the percentage of the church giving at higher levels. An effective way to measure progress is to compare your giving levels to the national average over a particular time period.

When I met representatives from MortarStone at the Christian Stewardship Network, they provided great information on tracking the right metrics for increasing generosity. Below are statistics on national average annual giving captured by MortarStone. You can request help interpreting your giving data or get more information at mortarstone.com.

National Average Annual Giving Units
by Category (MortarStone)

Level	Amount	Giving Units	Amount Given
Band 1	$1–$199	Not calculated	Not calculated
Band 2	$200–$999	43%	7%
Band 3	$1,000–$4,999	39%	29%
Band 4	$5,000–$9,999	12%	23%
Band 5	$10,000 or more	6%	41%

Below is Life Church data following the MortarStone-recommended categories.

Life Church Annual Giving Units by Category (2010)

Level	Amount	Giving Units	Amount Given	Avg. Annual Giving
Band 1	$1–$199	Not calculated	Not calculated	Not calculated
Band 2	$200–$999	47%	8%	Not calculated
Band 3	$1,000–$4,999	37%	31%	Not calculated
Band 4	$5,000–$9,999	10%	26%	Not calculated
Band 5	$10,000 or more	6%	35%	$16,457

Life Church Annual Giving Units by Category (2016)

Level	Amount	Giving Units	Amount Given	Avg. Annual Giving
Band 1	$1–$199	Not calculated	Not calculated	Not calculated
Band 2	$200–$999	41%	5%	Not calculated
Band 3	$1,000–$4,999	37%	23%	Not calculated
Band 4	$5,000–$9,999	12%	22%	Not calculated
Band 5	$10,000 or more	10%	50%	$20,403

These numbers may not seem like enormous increases, but they represent systemic changes in church culture. Over time, our church has a larger percentage of people giving at higher levels. This point is important. If the percentages of your church in the Band 4 and Band 5 categories are not increasing, you should question whether your processes for discipling people are really working.

We changed our church's giving culture significantly over the years. Our goal was to increase the percentage of givers in Band 4 and Band 5 categories and reduce the percentages in Band 2 and Band 3. As you see, we succeeded. We have increased Bands 4 and 5 givers from 16 percent to 22 percent. Our results exceed the national average of 18 percent for Bands 4 and 5. We also reduced Bands 1 and 2 givers from 84 percent to 78 percent.

We also saw average annual giving for Band 5 givers increase by 24 percent. When this increases year over year, it indicates we are getting more effective at engaging our highest-capacity givers and getting better at making disciples.

As I mentioned earlier, you should segment strategies to address each giving segment. The table below is an example of how to plan and measure impacts of these strategies by giving segment.

FOCUS ON THE GIVER, NOT THE GIFT

		Sample Discipleship Strategy by Giving Segment				
Segment	Description	# of Givers	$ Given	Giving %	Strategies	Resources
New Givers	Those with no prior history of giving to your general fund	875	$1,133,451	10%	Teach generous giving / Vision Partners in discovery	New members' team
					Biannual financial sermons with clear, direct money message	Lead pastor
					Send first-time givers note (weekly)	Accounting team
Trackable Givers	Those who have given to the general fund for at least twelve months *and* who give $200 or more annually	2,939	$11,421,477	99%	Hold leaders accountable to tithing	Pastors
					Invite potential Vision Partners to quarterly Vision Partners' events	Vision Partner champions
					Ninety-day tithe challenge	Lead pastor
					Write personal thank-you note to special large ($1,000 or more) gifts (weekly)	Pastors
					Offer regular stewardship education	Financial ministry team

	Sample Discipleship Strategy by Giving Segment					
Segment	**Description**	**# of Givers**	**$ Given**	**Giving %**	**Strategies**	**Resources**
Financial Leaders	Those who annually give $10,000 or more	281	$5,733,120	50%	Communicate compelling vision	Lead pastor
					Present annual vision offering	Lead pastor
					Meet one on one with Vision Partners and potential Vision Partners	Vision Partner champions
					Provide money coaching to key top givers	Stewardship pastor
					Vision Partner mission trips and outreach opportunities	Outreach/ missions pastor
					Monthly devotionals	Vision Partner champions
					Small group lunch gatherings with top givers	Vision Partner champions
					Vision update reports	Vision Partner admin

CONCLUSION

We have experienced significant results as we have focused on building a culture of generosity in our church and other churches. Again, here are just a few of our results we have seen:

- more financial resources available to do God's work
    - An annual vision offering can contribute an additional 20 percent to the general fund.
    - Ninety-five percent of Vision Partners give more than $2,000.

- stronger relationships/trust with givers
    - Money conversations aren't weird.
    - Rarely have top givers left the church.

- tangible growth with members both spiritually and in their personal finances
  - We have helped hundreds of members become homeowners, get out of debt, and succeed in business.
  - High number of salvation decisions during money series.

- unity in leadership toward a common vision
  - Almost every lay leader is a Vision Partner.
  - Vision Partners grow 20 percent more than church.

My hope is that you will experience the same or better results in your church. My prayer is that you become confident in having money discussions and money is not weird in your church. I pray that messages on money become a catalyst to help people make a decision for God and that you have more than enough financial resources to carry out the vision God has given you.

NOTES

1   John Maxwell, *The 21 Indispensable Qualities of a Leader* (Nashville: Thomas Nelson, 2007).

2   Bill and Belinda Gates, "Why Giving Away Our Wealth Has Been the Most Satisfying Thing We've Done," TED14, 2014.

3   Barna.com, "New Study Shows Trends in Tithing and Donating," 2008.

4   Jim Collins, *Good to Great* (New York: HarperCollins, 2001).

5   Janet Rae Dupree, "Can You Become a Creature of Habit?" *New York Times*, 2008.

6   Brian Tracy, *Maximum Achievement: Strategies and Skills That Will Unlock Your Hidden Power to Succeed* (New York: Fireside, 1995).

7   Jeff Anderson, *Plastic Donuts* (Acceptable Gift Inc., 2012).

8   Saul McLeod, *Skinner—Operant Conditioning*, www.simplypsychology.org, 2018.

9   MortarStone, https://mortarstone.com, 2019.